My

by Ruth Montgomery
illustrated by Anne-Sophie Lanquetin

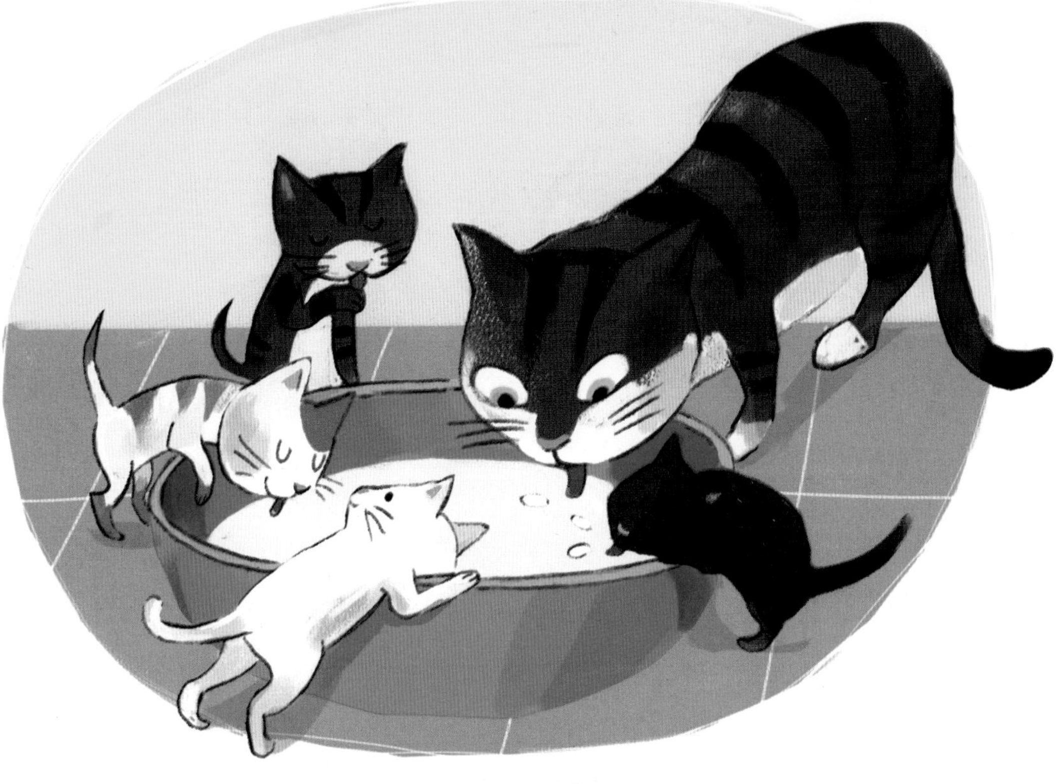

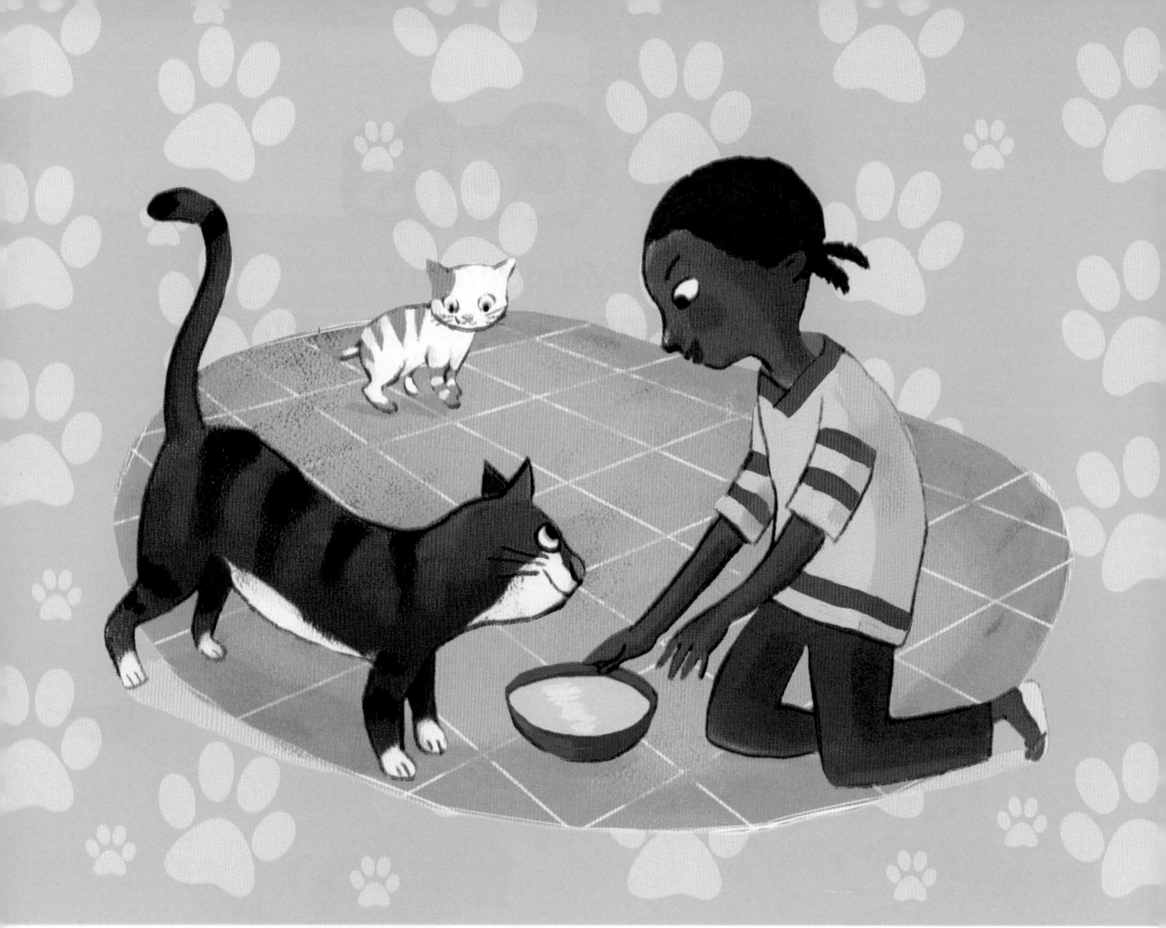

They get water.

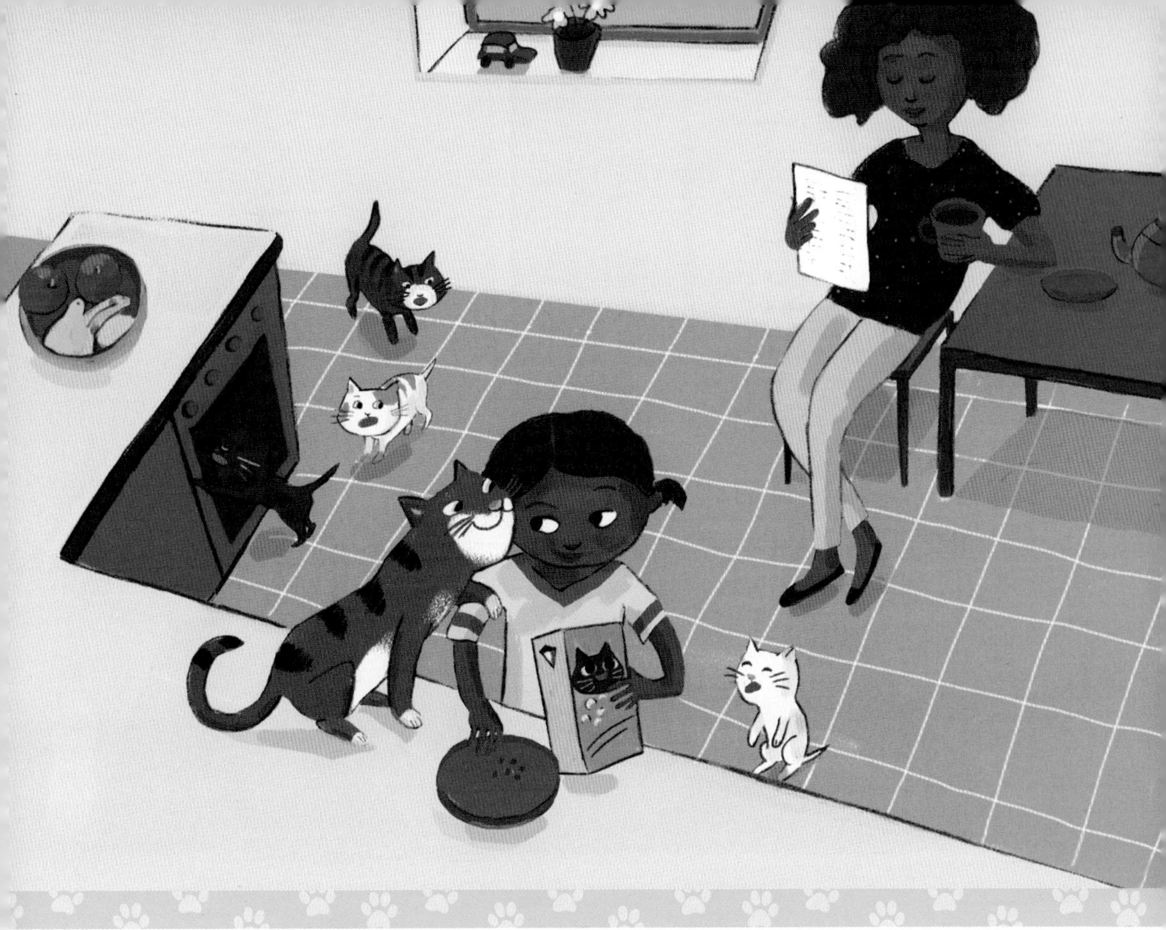

They get food.

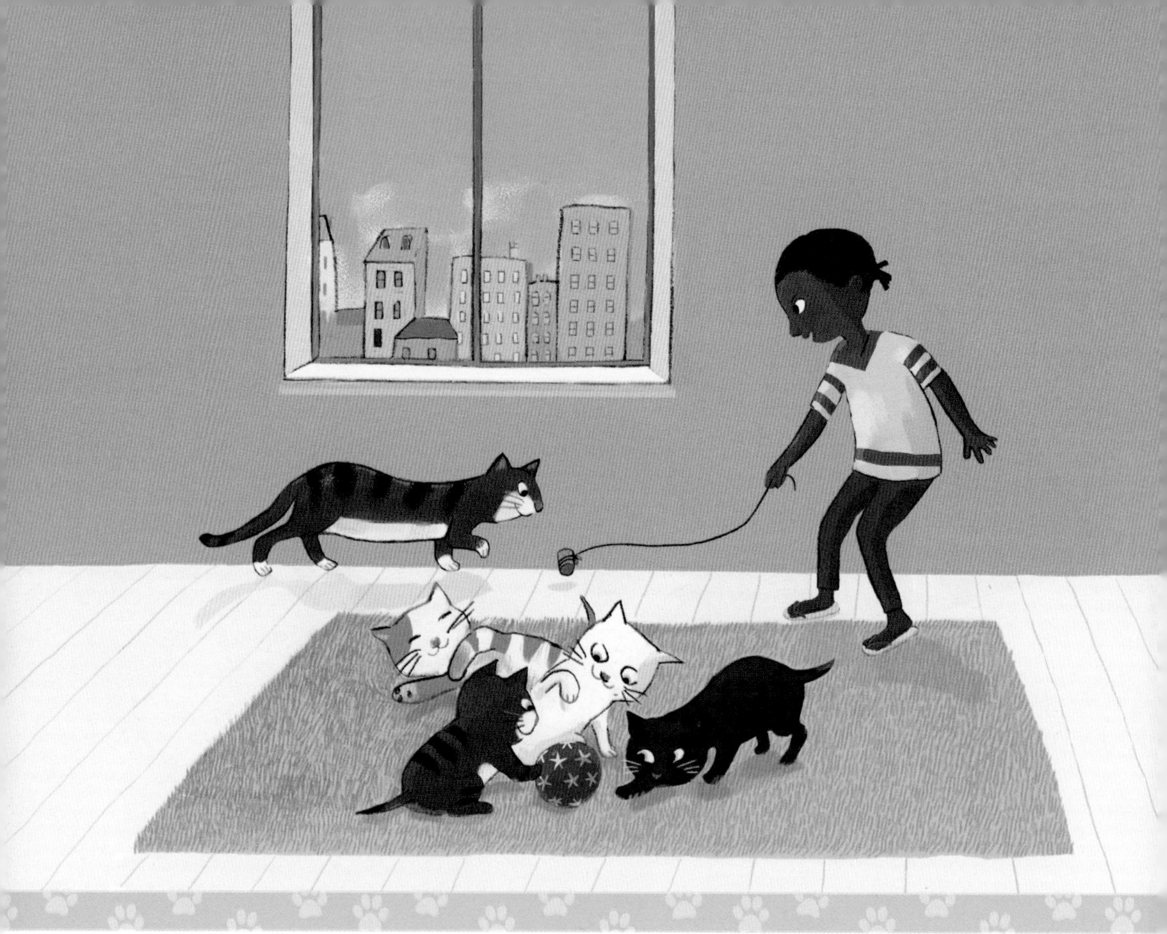

They get toys.

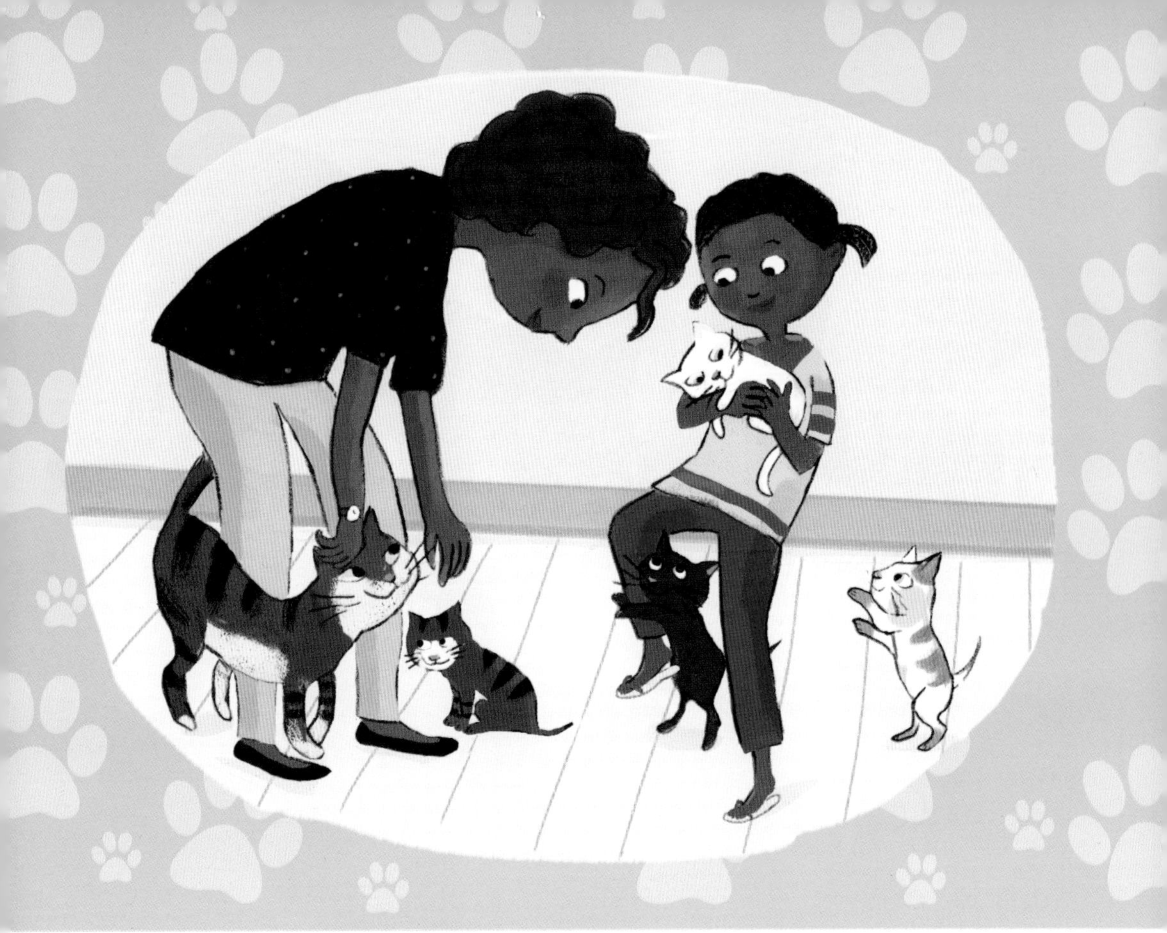

They get pats.

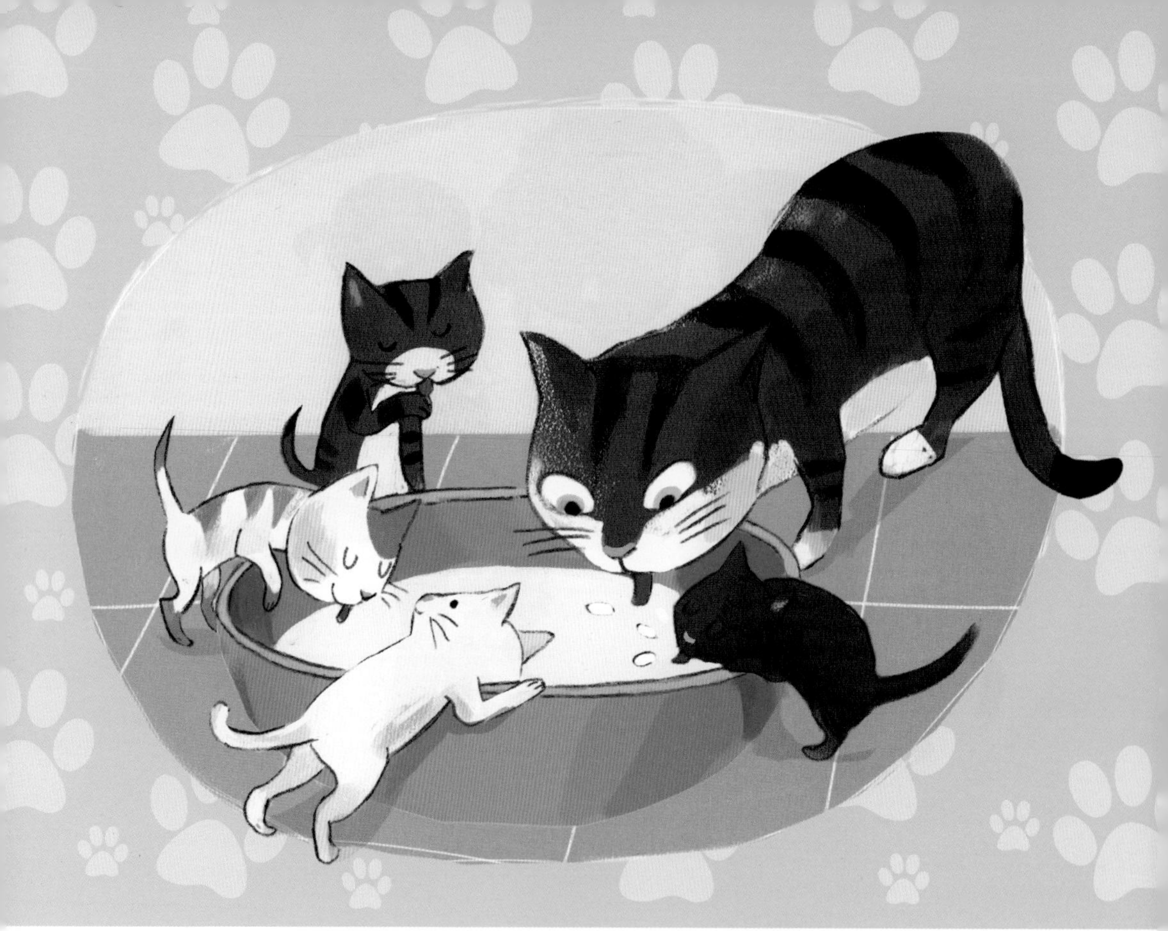

They get milk.

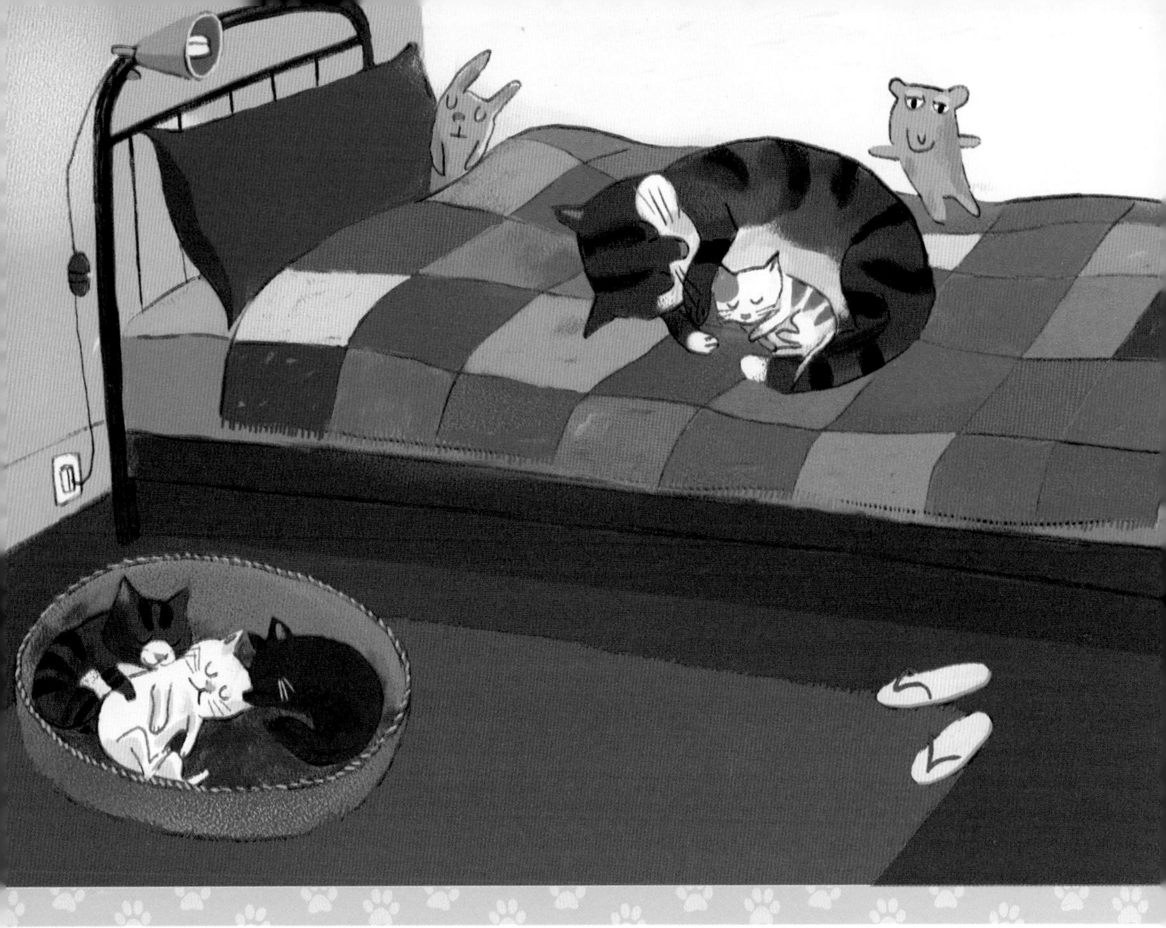

They get beds.

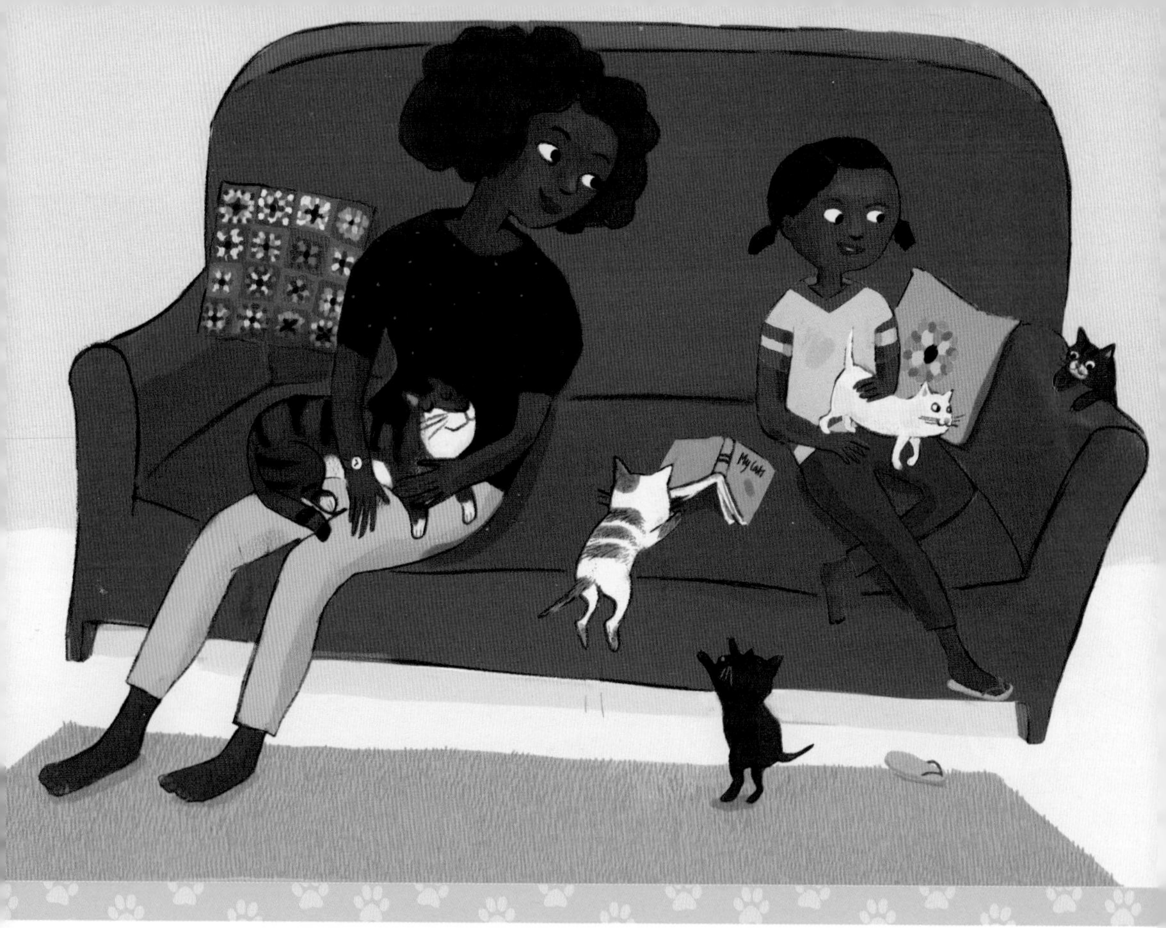

They get us!